MW00886841

HOLIDAY
PRESS

Instructions:

Starting on December 1st, complete one activity per day.

Have fun!

1

Create Bookish Art:

Illustrate a scene from your favorite book.

2

Write a letter to an author:

Pen a heartfelt letter to an author expressing your appreciation.

3

Host a book-themed picnic:

Pack a picnic inspired by a book's setting or characters.

4

Recreate a book cover:

Use household items to recreate a book cover and share it on social media.

5

Participate in a virtual book club meeting:

Join an online book club and engage in a virtual discussion.

6

Bookish playlist creation:

Compile a playlist inspired by the mood of a book or your favorite literary quotes.

7

Dress as a favorite character:

Spend the day dressed as a character from your favorite book.

8

Bookstore scavenger hunt:

Visit a bookstore and create a scavenger hunt based on book titles or genres.

9

Create a mini bookshelf display:

Arrange your books creatively on a shelf to showcase your favorites.

10

Write a book-related poem:

Compose a poem inspired by a book or a favorite literary theme.

11

Bookish movie marathon:

Watch film adaptations of your favorite books.

12

Create bookmarks:

Design personalized bookmarks with quotes and illustrations.

13

Organize a book swap with friends:

Exchange books with friends and discuss your choices.

14

Bookish baking challenge:

Bake treats inspired by books or characters.

15

Write a book review in 50 words:

Challenge yourself to condense your thoughts into a brief review.

16

Bookish trivia night:

Organize a trivia night with questions about your favorite books.

17

Visit a literary landmark online:

Take a virtual tour of a literary landmark or author's home.

18

Explore bookish podcasts:

Listen to podcasts discussing literature or author interviews.

19

Read a book in another language:

Challenge yourself by reading a book in a language you're learning.

20

Donate books to a Little Free Library:

Share your love of reading by donating books to a local Little Free Library.

21

Bookish karaoke night:

Sing songs related to books or literary themes.

22

Read a classic you haven’t read yet:

Explore a classic novel you haven't had the chance to read.

23

Read a book aloud:

Read a book aloud to a friend, family member, or yourself.

24

Read a book in a new location:

Take your book to a park, coffee shop, or another unique location.

25

Start a book journal:

Keep a journal where you jot down your thoughts about each book you read.

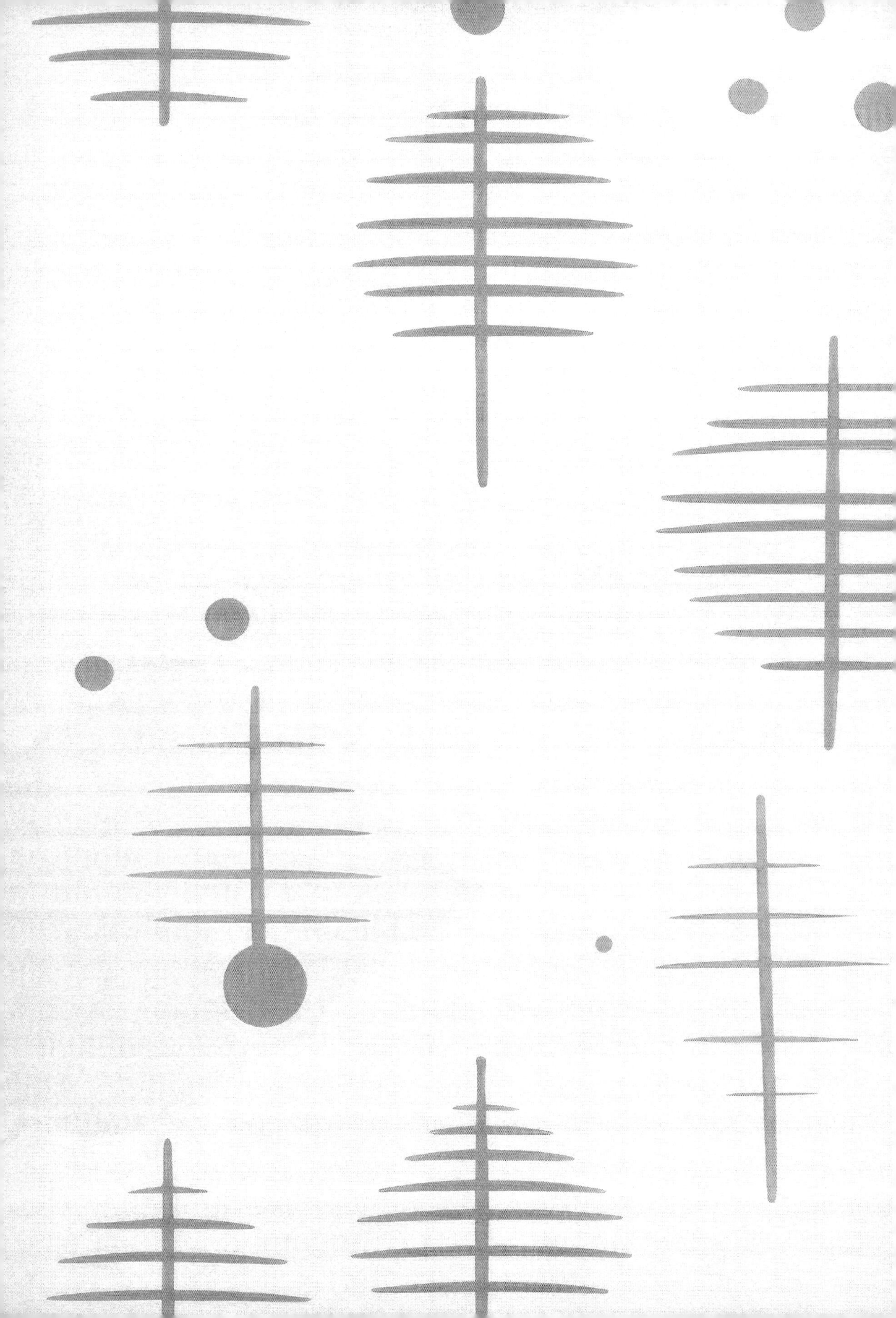

Reading Bucket List for the New Year:

1. ______________________________
2. ______________________________
3. ______________________________
4. ______________________________
5. ______________________________
6. ______________________________
7. ______________________________
8. ______________________________
9. ______________________________
10. ______________________________

Notes & Inspiration:

Thank you for purchasing!
If you liked this book, please
consider leaving a review.
We really appreciate your
feedback and it allows us to
reach more people.
Thank you!

Made in the USA
Monee, IL
23 September 2024